Whole Foods for Kids to Cook

La Leche League International

All rights reserved, including the right to reproduce this book
or portions thereof in any form.

This cookbook is a collection of favorite recipes,
which are not necessarily original recipes.

Published by La Leche League International

Copyright© 1995 La Leche League International
1400 North Meacham Road
Post Office Box 4079
Schaumburg, Illinois 60168-4079

Library of Congress Catalog Card Number: 95-077518
ISBN: 0-912500-46-8

Edited, Designed and Manufactured by:
Favorite Recipes® Press
P.O. Box 305142
Nashville, Tennessee 37230
1-800-358-0560

Manufactured in the United States of America
First Printing: 1995 7,500

Contents

Introduction

Since its beginning in 1956, La Leche League has emphasized the importance of healthy eating. Our mission is to help mothers breastfeed, and when babies start out at the breast, they are getting the best possible start nutritionally. Once other foods are introduced, parents naturally want their baby's diet to continue to focus on nutritious foods.

This cookbook, **Whole Foods for Kids to Cook**, goes the next step, into the stage when the toddler wants to "help." Preparing food and working in the kitchen provide an excellent atmosphere for learning as a child grows. Children are often willing to eat a much wider variety of foods when they are involved in the preparation.

The recipes in this cookbook have all been developed and submitted by La Leche League members and their children. They vary from recipes for preschoolers with only a few ingredients and simple directions, to those meant for children who have already developed some cooking skills. It's always a good idea for a parent to stay nearby whenever a child is using the stove, electrical appliances, or sharp knives. But remember that much of a child's enjoyment of cooking comes from the proud announcement, "I made it myself!"

We want to thank everyone who contributed recipes for this cookbook. Whether they were used or not, seeing the recipes that were submitted helped us develop the overall concept for the book.

We hope you enjoy sharing special times with your child and **Whole Foods for Kids to Cook**.

Judy Torgus
Executive Editor
La Leche League International

Beginning To Cook

Ants on a Log

Celery stalks
Peanut butter
Raisins

Tools . . . . table knife

Cut . . . . celery stalks into halves with knife.

Spread . . . . peanut butter on celery.

Arrange . . . . . . raisins on peanut butter.

Jane Fox, Ottawa, Ontario, Canada

Super Apple

1 popsicle stick
1 apple

Push . . . . popsicle stick carefully into bottom of apple.

Eat . . . . it like an apple popsicle.

Makes . . . . 1 serving.

Karen Golightly, Hamilton, Ontario, Canada

Apple Goodies

6 graham crackers
1 cup applesauce

Tools . . . . plastic bag with twist tie, measuring cup, 4 paper cups, spoon

Place . . . . graham crackers in plastic bag and seal with twist tie.

Squeeze . . . . . . bag with hands until crackers are crushed.

Layer . . . . applesauce and crumbs in paper cups with spoon until all are used.

Makes . . . . 4 servings.

Janice Knight Hartman, Millsboro, Delaware

Peanut Butter Apple

Apple
Peanut butter

Tools . . . . table knife, apple corer

Cut . . . . apple into halves.

Remove . . . . . . core with apple corer.

Fill . . . . center with peanut butter.

Makes . . . . 2 servings.

Joann Grohman, Dixfield, Maine

Banana-Berry Shakes

2 ripe bananas
1 to 2 cups fresh or frozen berries
2 cups milk or rice milk
1 cup yogurt, frozen yogurt or frozen rice milk
8 ice cubes

Tools . . . . measuring cup, blender, paper cups

Peel . . . . bananas and cut into chunks.

Combine . . . . . bananas with berries, milk, yogurt and ice cubes in blender.

Place . . . . cover on blender and blend until smooth.

Pour . . . . into paper cups.

Makes . . . . . . 4 servings.

Karen Herriot, Regina, Saskatchewan, Canada

Banana-Strawberry Yogurt Shake

1 whole banana, frozen
1/2 cup plain yogurt
3/4 cup milk
1 tablespoon strawberry or other jam (optional)

Tools . . . . table knife, measuring cup, measuring spoon, blender, tall glass, straw

Peel . . . . banana and cut into 1/2-inch slices.

Combine . . . . . banana with yogurt, milk and jam in blender.

Process . . . . . at high speed until smooth; ask an adult to help.

Pour . . . . into tall glass. Serve with a straw.

Makes . . . . 1 serving.

Joyce Thomson, Branford, Connecticut

Banana Boats

1 banana
2 tablespoons peanut butter
2 tablespoons coconut
1 tablespoon granola
Raisins, dates or other dried fruits

Tools . . . . table knife, measuring spoon

Peel . . . . banana and cut into halves lengthwise.

Spread . . . . peanut butter on cut sides of banana halves.

Sprinkle . . . . coconut, granola, raisins, dates or other fruits over peanut butter.

Share . . . . it with your sister or brother.

May . . . . press 2 sides of banana together and eat it all by yourself.

Makes . . . . 1 or 2 servings.

The Bromann Family, Glen Ellyn, Illinois
Carla Till, Rome, New York

Frozen Nutty Banana and Carob Chunks

1 teaspoon water
1 tablespoon carob powder
2 tablespoons honey
1/4 cup finely chopped almonds or other nuts
1 large banana, cut into 10 to 12 chunks

Tools . . . . measuring spoons, measuring cup, bowls, spoon, waxed paper, tray, table knife, fork, covered freezer-safe container

Combine . . . . . water, carob powder and honey in bowl with spoon; mix well.

Place . . . . almonds in small bowl.

Dip . . . . banana chunks into carob sauce and then into nuts using fork and spoon.

Arrange . . . . . on waxed paper-lined tray.

Freeze . . . . for 2 to 3 hours or until firm.

Store . . . . in covered container in freezer.

Makes . . . . 2 servings.

Chris Mayou, Onalaska, Wisconsin

Banana Cakes

Bananas
Peanut butter

Peel . . . . bananas and cut into rounds.

Spoon . . . . a dab of peanut butter onto each round.

Place . . . . another banana round on top of the peanut butter.

D.D. and Jackie MacKinnon, Quebec, Canada

Butter

1 cup whipping cream
1 pinch of salt

Tools . . . . measuring cup, pint jar with screw lid, spoon, bowl

Pour . . . . cream into jar and cover tightly.

Shake . . . . jar until butter separates from cream and forms a lump.

Remove . . . . butter to bowl. The liquid left in the jar is buttermilk.

Add . . . . salt to butter and mix well.

Serve . . . . on bread or crackers.

Heidi Gleber, East Bloomfield, New York

Frozen Grapes

Seedless grape clusters

Tools . . . . freezer-safe bowl

Pick . . . . grapes off stems and place in freezer-safe bowl.

Freeze . . . . . . until firm.

Eat . . . . as a snack—especially good on a hot day.

The Meeks Family, Houston, Texas

Gorp

1 cup peanuts
1 cup raisins
1 cup sunflower seeds
1 cup each Bran Chex, Wheat Chex and Corn Chex

Tools . . . . measuring cup, plastic container with lid, spoon

Combine . . . . . peanuts, raisins, sunflower seeds and cereal in plastic container and mix well with spoon.

Cover . . . . with lid to store.

Makes . . . . . . 15 servings.

Swiss Birchermuesli

2 cups liquid such as milk, yogurt, soya drink, juice or cashew cream
2 cups rolled oats
1/4 cup seeds such as sesame seeds, pumpkin seeds, sunflower seeds or linseeds
1/2 cup raisins or other dried fruits
1 apple, finely grated
Sugar to taste

Tools . . . . measuring cup, bowl, spoon

Combine . . . . . liquid and oats in bowl; mix well with spoon.

Add . . . . seeds, raisins and apple; mix well.

Taste . . . . muesli and add sugar if needed.

May . . . . also add bran or wheat germ.

Makes . . . . . . 10 servings.

Heidi Kuonen-Goetz, Switzerland

Fruit Dip

1 cup sour cream
1 tablespoon sugar
1 teaspoon cinnamon

Tools . . . . measuring cup, bowl, measuring spoons, mixing spoon

Combine . . . . . sour cream, sugar and cinnamon in bowl; mix well with spoon.

Serve . . . . with fruit to dip.

Makes . . . . 8 servings.

Sarah and Allan Meeks, Houston, Texas

Peanut Butter Dip

1 cup peanut butter
1 cup plain yogurt
1/4 cup unsweetened coconut

Tools . . . . measuring cup, bowl, spoon

Combine . . . . . peanut butter, yogurt and coconut in bowl; mix well with spoon.

Serve . . . . with vegetables such as carrots, celery, cucumbers or cauliflower to dip.

Makes . . . . 12 servings.

Nancy Johnson, Greeley, Colorado

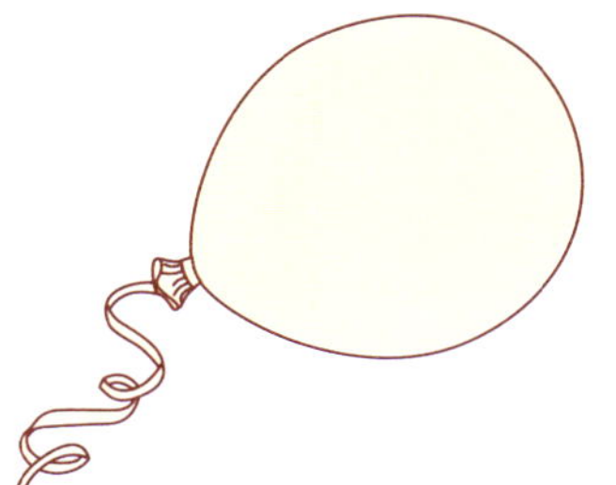

Guacamole

2 avocados
3 tablespoons salsa
2 tablespoons lemon juice or lime juice
1 clove of garlic, mashed, or garlic salt to taste
1 green onion, chopped
2 tablespoons finely chopped cilantro

Tools . . . . table knife, bowl, fork, measuring spoon

Peel . . . . avocados with table knife, reserving pits.

Mash . . . . avocados coarsely in bowl with fork.

Add . . . . salsa, lemon juice, garlic, green onion and cilantro, mixing well.

Place . . . . pits in guacamole to prevent browning.

Chill . . . . for 1 hour or longer.

May . . . . adjust amounts of seasonings to suit your taste, taking care not to make it runny.

Makes . . . . 12 servings.

Beatriz Aguirre Haymer, Honolulu, Hawaii

Little Dippers

Whole grain bagels
Bananas
Natural peanut butter

Tools . . . . table knife, bowl, fork, plate

Cut . . . . bagels into bite-size pieces.

Peel . . . . bananas and mash in bowl with fork.

Add . . . . peanut butter and mix well.

Place . . . . bowl in center of plate and arrange bagel bites around bowl.

The Bromann Family, Glen Ellyn, Illinois

Big Dippers

2 to 3 tablespoons honey
1/3 to 1/2 cup peanut butter
Hard or soft whole grain pretzels

Tools . . . . measuring spoon, measuring bowl, mixing spoon, plate

Mix . . . . honey and peanut butter in bowl with fork.

Place . . . . bowl in center of plate and arrange pretzels around bowl.

May . . . . keep soft pretzels warm in slow cooker set on Low.

The Bromann Family, Glen Ellyn, Illinois

Honey Crunch Popcorn

6 quarts popped popcorn
2 cups nuts
1 cup butter
1 cup honey

Tools . . . . measuring cup, bowl, spoon, saucepan, baking sheets, potholders

Ask . . . . an adult to preheat the oven to 350 degrees.

Mix . . . . popcorn and nuts in large bowl.

Combine . . . . . butter and honey in saucepan.

Heat . . . . until butter melts, stirring with spoon to mix well; ask an adult to help.

Pour . . . . over the popcorn and stir to mix well.

Spread . . . . mixture on baking sheets.

Bake . . . . for 10 to 15 minutes, stirring occasionally.

Remove . . . . from oven with potholders.

Let . . . . stand until cool and crunchy.

Makes . . . . 24 servings.

Holiday Spiced Popcorn

2 tablespoons melted butter
2 tablespoons honey
8 cups popped popcorn
1 teaspoon pumpkin pie spice

Tools . . . . measuring spoons, small bowl, spoon, measuring cup, large bowl

Combine . . . . . butter and honey in small bowl and mix well with spoon.

Pour . . . . over popcorn in large bowl; mix well.

Sprinkle . . . . . with pumpkin pie spice and mix well.

May . . . . package in small bags to give at Halloween, parties or holidays.

Makes . . . . 8 servings.

Chris Mayou, Onalaska. Wisconsin

Piggyback Peanut Butter and Jelly Sandwich

Natural peanut butter
All-fruit jelly
3 slices thinly sliced whole grain bread

Tools . . . . table knife, plate

Spread . . . . . . peanut butter and jelly on 2 pieces of bread.

Stack . . . . the spread pieces of bread on plate.

Top . . . . with the remaining piece of bread.

Makes . . . . 1 serving.

The Bromann Family, Glen Ellyn, Illinois

Shaped Cheese Sandwich

2 slices bread
1 slice cheese

Tools . . . . cookie cutter

Cut . . . . bread with cookie cutter in any shape you like.

Cut . . . . cheese with the same cookie cutter.

Place . . . . cheese between slices of bread.

May . . . . freeze bread to make it easier to cut if you can wait for it to thaw before eating the sandwich.

Makes . . . . 1 serving.

Shelley Houvener, Warren, Michigan

Just Cheese, Please, Pizzas

1 whole wheat pita round or English muffin
Shredded mozzarella cheese

Tools . . . . table knife, baking sheet, potholders

Ask . . . . an adult to preheat the oven to 425 degrees.

Cut . . . . pita round or muffin horizontally into 2 halves.

Place . . . . cut side up on baking sheet.

Sprinkle . . . . . with cheese.

Bake . . . . for 10 to 15 minutes or until cheese is bubbly.

Remove . . . . . from oven with potholders; ask an adult to help.

Makes . . . . 2 servings.

The Bromann Family, Glen Ellyn, Illinois

Easy Tuna Burgers

1 (7-ounce) can tuna, drained
Mayonnaise
3 hamburger buns
6 slices cheese

Tools . . . . can opener, spoon, baking sheet, potholders

Ask . . . . an adult to preheat the broiler.

Open . . . . tuna and spoon into bowl.

Add . . . . enough mayonnaise to make a spread and mix well with spoon.

Spread . . . . tuna mixture onto cut sides of hamburger buns.

Place . . . . on baking sheet.

Top . . . . with 1 slice of cheese.

Broil . . . . until cheese melts.

Remove . . . . from oven with potholders; ask an adult to help.

Makes . . . . 6 servings.

Heidi Gleber, East Bloomfield, New York

UFOs (Unidentified Frying Objects)

1 slice whole grain bread
1 tablespoon butter
1 egg
Salt and pepper to taste

Tools . . . . round cookie cutter, table knife, skillet, pancake turner, potholders

Cut . . . . hole in center of bread with round cookie cutter.

Spread . . . . half the butter on 1 side of the bread slice and cut-out-hole with table knife.

Melt . . . . remaining butter in skillet; ask an adult to help with the stove.

Place . . . . bread slice and cut-out-hole in butter in skillet.

Fry . . . . until brown on the bottom. Turn with a pancake turner.

Break . . . . egg into the hole in the bread and sprinkle with salt and pepper.

Cook . . . . until egg begins to set.

Turn . . . . bread again with pancake turner.

Cook . . . . just until other side is set.

Makes . . . . 1 serving.

Rita Lare, Akron, Ohio
Diana Reardon, Dallas, Texas

Banana Split Sandwich

2 to 3 tablespoons peanut butter
1 thick slice of whole wheat bread, half a pita, or leftover pancake
1/2 banana, sliced
Honey or natural fruit syrup to taste
1 tablespoon sunflower seeds
1 tablespoon unsweetened coconut

Tools . . . . measuring spoon, table knife

Spread . . . . . . peanut butter on bread with table knife.

Arrange . . . . . . banana slices on peanut butter.

Drizzle . . . . . . with honey.

Sprinkle . . . . . . with sunflower seeds and coconut.

Makes . . . . . . 1 serving.

Chris Mayou, Onalaska, Wisconsin

Honey-Almond Rice Cakes

Honey
Plain rice cake
Finely ground almonds

Tools . . . . spoon, plate

Drizzle . . . . . . honey on rice cake with spoon.

Spread . . . . . . almonds on small plate.

Press . . . . rice cake honey side down in almonds.

Shake . . . . off excess almonds.

Makes . . . . 1 serving.

The Bromann Family, Glen Ellyn, Illinois

Peanut Butter Roll-Ups

Peanut butter
4 flour tortillas
Sunflower seeds, dried fruit bits, sliced banana or raisins

Tools . . . . table knife

Spread . . . . . . peanut butter on 1 side of each tortilla.

Sprinkle . . . . . with sunflower seeds or other toppings of choice.

Roll . . . . up to enclose filling.

May . . . . slice tortillas into bite-size treats if preferred.

Makes . . . . 4 servings.

Karen Herriot, Regina, Saskatchewan, Canada

Quick and Easy Soup

3 potatoes, peeled or unpeeled
4 carrots
2 cups (or more) mushrooms
3 chicken bouillon cubes
3 cups water

Tools . . . . knife, measuring cup, saucepan, potholders

Ask . . . . an adult to help wash and cut up the potatoes, carrots and mushrooms into small pieces.

Combine . . . . . bouillon cubes, water and potatoes in saucepan.

Bring . . . . to a boil and add carrots; ask an adult to help.

Bring . . . . to a boil and add mushrooms.

Simmer . . . . . . covered, for 20 to 30 minutes longer or until vegetables are tender.

Makes . . . . 3 to 4 servings.

Marianne Vakiener, Fairfax, Virginia

Crunchy Soup

Carrot, spinach or other vegetable that can be eaten raw
Water

Tools . . . . saucepan, table knife, spoon

Fill . . . . saucepan halfway with water.

Tear . . . . or cut vegetable into bite-size pieces.

Add . . . . to the water and stir with spoon.

Ask . . . . your friends to help you eat it right out of the saucepan.

D.D. and Jackie MacKinnon, Quebec, Canada

Tangy Beet Salad

4 whole beets
Water
Juice of 1 lemon or to taste

Tools . . . . saucepan, potholders, table knife, bowl, jar with cover

Combine . . . . . whole beets with water to cover in saucepan.

Cook . . . . until beets are tender and drain; ask an adult to help.

Cool . . . . beets in a pan of cold water and drain again.

Peel . . . . beets with fingers.

Slice . . . . beets into bowl.

Squeeze . . . . . lemon juice over beets.

Store . . . . in covered jar in refrigerator.

May . . . . substitute vinegar for lemon juice.

Makes . . . . 4 servings.

Karen Golightly, Hamilton, Ontario, Canada

Baked Potatoes

2 medium potatoes

Tools . . . . fork, paper towel, potholders

Pierce . . . . . . potatoes with fork.

Place . . . . on paper towel in microwave.

Microwave . . . . on High for 12 to 15 minutes or until tender.

Remove . . . . . potatoes from microwave with potholder; ask an adult to help.

Makes . . . . . . 2 servings.

The Meeks Family, Houston, Texas

Potato Head

1 potato
Olives, small pieces of fruits and vegetables

Tools . . . . fork, potholder, wooden toothpicks

Ask . . . . an adult to preheat the oven to 400 degrees.

Pierce . . . . . . potato with fork.

Bake . . . . for 30 to 40 minutes or until tender. Remove with a potholder and cool.

Make . . . . eyes, ears, nose, mouth, eyebrows, hair and hat with olives and pieces of fruits and vegetables, securing with wooden picks.

Let . . . . your imagination loose; make a Carmen Miranda hat of fruit, for example.

Makes . . . . . . 1 serving.

The Bromann Family, Glen Ellyn, Illinois

Apple-Snapple Porridge

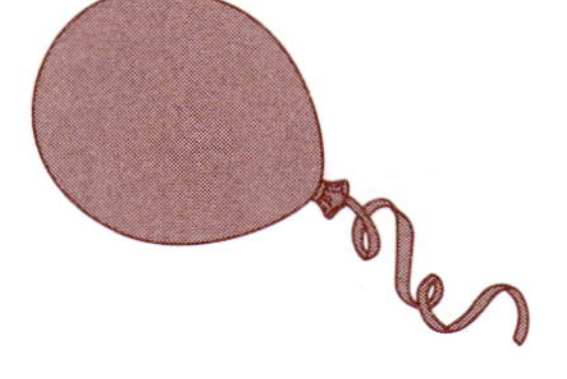

1 medium apple
3 cups apple juice
$1\frac{1}{3}$ cups rolled oats
$\frac{1}{4}$ cup raisins
$\frac{1}{4}$ teaspoon cinnamon
Milk and brown sugar or unsweetened coconut

Tools . . . . knife, measuring cup, measuring spoon, saucepan, potholders

Slice . . . . and chop the apple, discarding the core.

Combine . . . . . with apple juice, oats, raisins and cinnamon in saucepan.

Cook . . . . over medium-high heat until bubbly, stirring occasionally; ask an adult to help.

Reduce . . . . . . heat and simmer for 5 minutes longer.

Top . . . . with milk and a sprinkle of brown sugar or coconut.

Makes . . . . . . 4 servings.

Karen Herriot, Regina, Saskatchewan, Canada

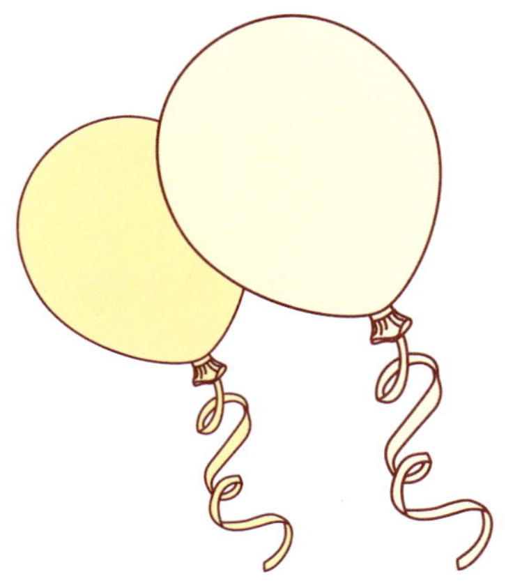

Edibowls

$^{1}/_{2}$ cup natural peanut butter, at room temperature
3 tablespoons butter, softened, or cold-pressed canola oil
$^{1}/_{3}$ cup honey
6 rice cakes
Yogurt or fruit

Tools . . . . measuring cup, measuring spoon, bowl, spoon, blender or food processor, muffin cups, table knife

Combine . . . . . peanut butter, butter and honey in a bowl and mix well with spoon.

Process . . . . . rice cakes a few at a time in blender or food processor until ground.

Add . . . . to the peanut butter mixture; mix well.

Press . . . . into greased muffin cups with greased fingers.

Chill . . . . in refrigerator until firm.

Remove . . . . . edibowls from muffin cups with knife.

Fill . . . . with yogurt or fruit.

Makes . . . . 8 servings.

The Bromann Family, Glen Ellyn, Illinois

Fruit and Rice Dessert

2 cups cooked rice, chilled
1/2 cup chopped dates or other chopped dried fruit
1/2 cup chopped nuts
1/2 cup sunflower seeds (optional)
1 cup drained crushed pineapple
2 tablespoons honey

Tools . . . . measuring cups, measuring spoon, bowl, spoon

Combine . . . . . rice, dates, nuts, sunflower seeds, pineapple and honey in bowl and mix well with spoon.

Chill . . . . in refrigerator.

May . . . . serve with fresh berries or whipped cream for a company dessert.

Makes . . . . 6 servings.

Chris Mayou, Onalaska, Wisconsin

Quick Rice Pudding

1/4 cup cooked brown rice
1 cup vanilla yogurt
1/4 cup raisins or coconut
Cinnamon to taste

Tools . . . . measuring cup, bowl, spoon

Combine . . . . . rice, yogurt, raisins or coconut and cinnamon in bowl and mix well with spoon.

Makes . . . . . . 1 serving.

Heidi Gleber, East Bloomfield, New York

Gelatin Shapes

10 envelopes unflavored gelatin
3 cups water
16 ounces apple or cranberry juice concentrate

Tools . . . . measuring cup, spoon, saucepan, cookie cutters

Stir . . . . gelatin into water in saucepan and let stand until softened.

Heat . . . . until gelatin dissolves, stirring constantly; ask an adult to help.

Add . . . . juice; mix well. Pour into flat dish.

Chill . . . . until firm.

Cut . . . . into desired shapes with cookie cutters.

Makes . . . . . . 20 or more shapes.

The Meeks Family, Houston, Texas

Banana Popsicles

4 large bananas
Apple juice

Tools . . . . table knife, popsicle sticks, popsicle molds

Peel . . . . bananas and cut into halves.

Place . . . . 1 popsicle stick into cut end of each banana and place in popsicle mold.

Pour . . . . apple juice into molds around bananas.

Freeze . . . . . . until firm.

Makes . . . . . . 8 servings.

Graham Boyes, Vancouver, British Columbia, Canada

Creamsicles

1 (6-ounce) can frozen orange juice concentrate, thawed
32 ounces plain yogurt

Tools . . . . bowl, spoon, popsicle molds, popsicle sticks

Mix . . . . orange juice concentrate and yogurt in bowl with spoon.

Spoon . . . . . . into popsicle molds.

Place . . . . popsicle stick into each mold.

Freeze . . . . . . until firm.

May . . . . stir orange juice lightly into yogurt to make a swirled effect.

Makes . . . . . . 8 or 9 servings.

Muriel Pellegrino, Stoughton, Massachusetts

Fudgesicles

3/4 cup chopped dates
2 cups warm water
1/2 cup milk, soy milk powder or 1/4 cup milk powder and 1/4 cup protein powder
3/4 cup walnuts or other nuts
2 tablespoons carob powder
2 teaspoons vanilla extract

Tools . . . . measuring cup, bowl, measuring spoons, blender, popsicle molds, popsicle sticks

Soak . . . . dates in warm water in bowl for 30 minutes.

Combine . . . . . date mixture with milk, walnuts, carob powder and vanilla in blender.

Process . . . . . until smooth; ask an adult to help.

Pour . . . . into popsicle molds.

Insert . . . . popsicle sticks into molds.

Freeze . . . . until firm.

Makes . . . . 16 servings.

Kaitlin Wiebe, La Riviere, Manitoba, Canada

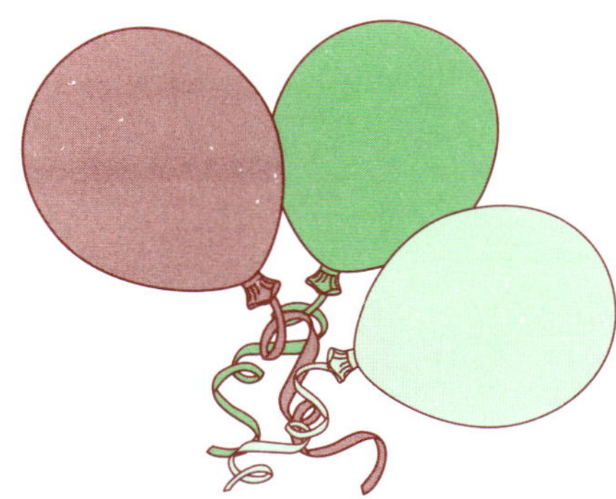

Carob Fudge Balls

1 cup sesame butter (tahini)
$^1/_4$ cup raw carob powder
1 tablespoon raw honey
$^1/_4$ teaspoon vanilla extract
1 cup raisins
$^1/_2$ cup shredded unsweetened coconut

Tools . . . . measuring cup, measuring spoons, bowl, spoon

Combine . . . . . sesame butter, carob powder, honey and vanilla in bowl and mix well with spoon.

Stir . . . . in raisins and coconut.

Shape . . . . into balls.

Store . . . . in refrigerator or freezer.

Makes . . . . 32 balls.

Denise Fidler, Syracuse, Indiana

Honey Nut Balls

1 cup peanut butter
1/2 cup honey
1 teaspoon vanilla extract
1 cup raisins
1/2 cup chopped nuts
1/2 to 1 1/2 cups shredded coconut

Tools . . . . measuring cup, measuring spoon, bowl, spoon, waxed paper, plate

Combine . . . . . peanut butter, honey and vanilla in bowl and mix well with spoon.

Stir . . . . in raisins and nuts.

Shape . . . . into very small balls.

Sprinkle . . . . . coconut onto waxed paper.

Roll . . . . balls in coconut, coating well.

Place . . . . on plate.

Chill . . . . in refrigerator for 3 hours.

Makes . . . . 48 balls.

Margaret J. Black, Rome, Italy

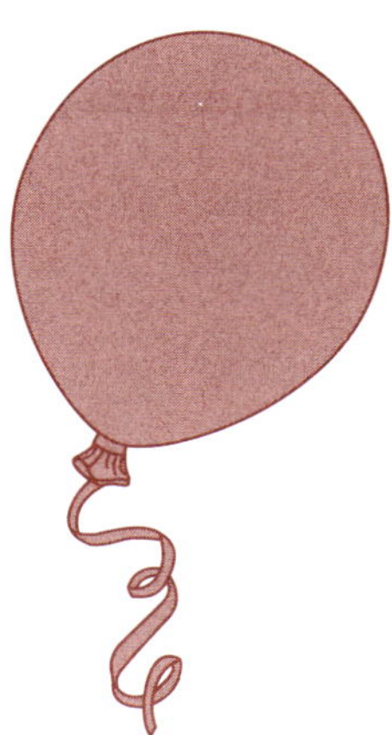

Peanut Butter and Raisin Balls

2 tablespoons honey
1 cup peanut butter
1 tablespoon butter, softened
3/4 cup dry milk powder
1/2 cup chopped nuts
1 cup raisins
Graham cracker crumbs

Tools . . . . measuring spoon, measuring cup, bowl, spoon, waxed paper

Combine . . . . . honey, peanut butter and butter in bowl and mix well with spoon.

Add . . . . milk powder, nuts and raisins; mix well.

Shape . . . . into balls.

Sprinkle . . . . . . graham cracker crumbs onto waxed paper.

Roll . . . . balls in graham cracker crumbs.

May . . . . freeze if desired.

Makes . . . . 32 balls.

Denise Fidler, Syracuse, Indiana

Peanut Butter Balls

1¼ cups crunchy peanut butter
½ cup honey
1 teaspoon vanilla extract
1¼ cups dry milk powder

Tools . . . . measuring cup, measuring spoon, food processor

Combine . . . . . peanut butter, honey and vanilla in food processor container.

Process . . . . . until smooth; ask an adult to help.

Add . . . . milk powder gradually, processing constantly until thick.

Shape . . . . into balls.

Makes . . . . 32 balls.

The Meeks Family, Houston, Texas

Crunchy Peanut Butter Balls

1 tablespoon peanut butter
1/2 teaspoon honey
2 teaspoon dry milk powder
8 Wheat Chex or other wheat or rice cereal

Tools . . . . measuring spoons, bowl, spoon, sealable plastic bag, rolling pin

Combine . . . . . peanut butter and honey in bowl and mix well with spoon.

Add . . . . dry milk powder; mix well.

Place . . . . Wheat Chex into plastic bag and crush with rolling pin.

Shape . . . . peanut butter mixture by teaspoonfuls into balls.

Shake . . . . in crushed cereal in plastic bag, coating well.

Makes . . . . 2 servings.

Kim and Hannah Brinson, Fayetteville, Arkansas

No-Bake Carob and Orange Treats

1/4 cup carob powder
2 cups finely crushed graham crackers or whole grain cookies
1 1/2 cups finely chopped walnuts or other nuts
1/4 cup honey
1/3 cup orange juice or apple juice

Tools . . . . measuring cup, bowl, spoon, waxed paper, plate

Combine . . . . . carob powder, graham cracker crumbs and half the walnuts in bowl and mix well with spoon.

Add . . . . honey and juice and mix well.

Shape . . . . into balls.

Sprinkle . . . . . remaining walnuts on waxed paper.

Roll . . . . balls in walnuts, coating well.

Place . . . . on plate.

Store . . . . in refrigerator.

May . . . . crush crackers in food processor with an adult's help.

Makes . . . . 48 treats.

Chris Mayou, Onalaska, Wisconsin

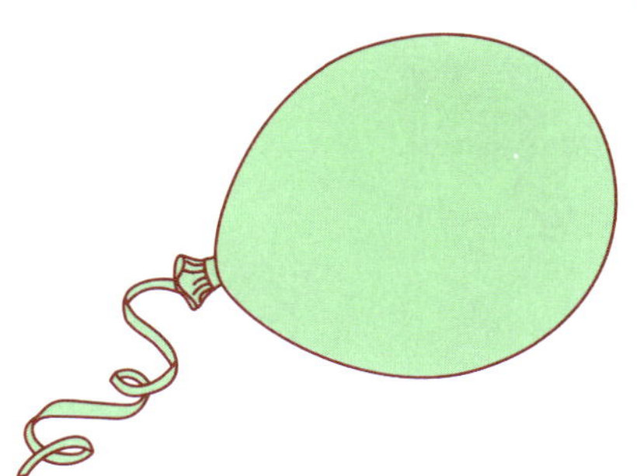

Edible Peanut Butter Play Dough

1 cup smooth peanut butter
1 cup honey or molasses
2 cups (or more) dry milk powder
Sunflower seeds, raisins or coconut

Tools . . . . measuring cup, bowl, spoon, cookie cutters

Combine . . . . . peanut butter, honey and 2 cups dry milk powder in bowl and mix well with spoon.

Knead . . . . on surface sprinkled with additional dry milk powder, kneading in milk powder if needed to form dough.

Shape . . . . dough into desired shapes or roll and cut into desired shapes.

Sprinkle . . . . . . or decorate with sunflower seeds, raisins or coconut if desired.

Makes . . . . 32 treats.

Carolyn Pennington, House Springs, Missouri

Peanut Butter Surprises

½ cup peanut butter
1 tablespoon honey
⅓ cup dry milk powder
2 tablespoons sesame seeds
2 tablespoons wheat germ
½ cup cornflakes or coconut
25 raisins or peanuts

Tools . . . . measuring cup, measuring spoon, bowl, spoon, sealable plastic bag, rolling pin

Combine . . . . . peanut butter and honey in bowl and mix well with spoon.

Add . . . . milk powder, sesame seeds and wheat germ; mix well.

Place . . . . cornflakes or coconut in plastic bag and seal bag.

Crush . . . . cereal with rolling pin or hands.

Sprinkle . . . . . cereal onto waxed paper.

Shape . . . . peanut butter mixture by teaspoonfuls around a raisin or peanut with greased hands.

Roll . . . . in cereal or coconut.

Makes . . . . 25 balls.

Karen Herriot, Regina, Saskatchewan, Canada

Crispy Squares

1 cup smooth peanut butter
1/2 cup honey
1 cup dry milk powder
2 to 4 cups toasted rice cereal

Tools . . . . measuring cup, bowl, spoon, 8x8-inch pan

Combine . . . . . . peanut butter and honey in bowl and mix well with spoon.

Add . . . . milk powder and mix well.

Mix . . . . in desired amount of cereal with hands.

Press . . . . into 8x8-inch pan.

Chill . . . . in refrigerator.

Cut . . . . into squares.

Makes . . . . 16 servings.

Mary Murphy, North Canton, Ohio

Now You're Cooking

Pot of Gold Mulled Cider

2 quarts apple juice or apple cider
1/4 to 1/2 cup orange juice (optional)
1/4 to 1/2 cup packed brown sugar
1 teaspoon allspice
1 1/2 teaspoons ground cloves
1 1/2 teaspoons cinnamon
1 lemon or orange, sliced (optional)

Tools . . . . measuring cup, measuring spoon, slow cooker, spoon

Combine . . . . . apple juice, orange juice, brown sugar, allspice, cloves, cinnamon and lemon or orange slices in slow cooker and mix well with spoon.

Heat . . . . on Low for 2 to 8 hours.

Ladle . . . . into mugs to serve; ask an adult to help.

Makes . . . . 8 servings.

Chris Mayou, Onalaska, Wisconsin

Granola

5 cups rolled oats
1 cup wheat germ
1 cup unsweetened shredded coconut
1 cup unblanched sliced almonds
1 cup raw sunflower seeds
1/2 cup unhulled sesame seeds
3/4 cup vegetable oil
3/4 cup honey

Tools . . . . measuring cup, roasting pan, bowl, spoon, potholders

Preheat . . . . . oven to 325 degrees.

Mix . . . . oats, wheat germ, coconut, almonds, sunflower seeds and sesame seeds in roasting pan.

Combine . . . . . oil and honey in bowl and mix well with spoon.

Pour . . . . over oats mixture, mixing well.

Bake . . . . for 30 to 60 minutes or until light brown and dry, stirring every 15 minutes.

Serve . . . . as a crunchy snack, mixed with applesauce or yogurt, with milk for breakfast, or sprinkled over fruit, yogurt or ice cream for dessert.

Makes . . . . 9 1/2 cups.

The LeMay Family, Eau Claire, Wisconsin

Quesadillas

1 corn or flour tortilla
Shredded Monterey Jack, Cheddar, mozzarella or other kind of cheese

Tools . . . . nonstick griddle or skillet, pancake turner

Place . . . . tortilla on hot griddle.

Sprinkle . . . . . . cheese over half the tortilla.

Fold . . . . remaining side of tortilla over cheese.

Cook . . . . until cheese melts and tortilla is light brown on both sides, turning once with pancake turner.

Remove . . . . . . to plate. Cut into smaller pieces if desired.

Serve . . . . warm or cold, but watch out for hot cheese.

Makes . . . . . . 1 serving.

Beatriz Aguirre Haymer, Honolulu, Hawaii

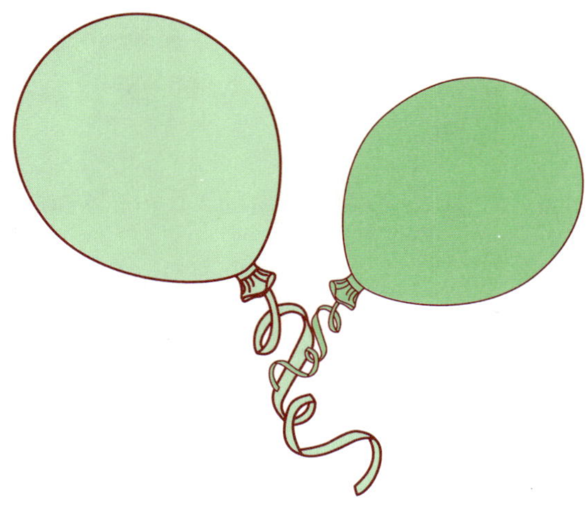

Turkey Jerky

1 to 2 pounds boneless turkey breast
1/4 cup soy sauce
1/4 cup Worcestershire sauce
1 teaspoon minced onion
1/4 teaspoon garlic powder
1/4 teaspoon salt

Tools . . . . knife, shallow baking pan, measuring cup, measuring spoon, bowl, spoon

Rinse . . . . turkey and pat dry.

Cut . . . . turkey into 1/4-inch strips and arrange in single layer in shallow baking pan.

Combine . . . . . soy sauce, Worcestershire sauce, onion, garlic powder and salt in bowl and mix well with spoon.

Pour . . . . over turkey and mix to coat well.

Marinate . . . . in refrigerator for 6 to 8 hours, stirring occasionally.

Preheat . . . . . oven to 150 degrees.

Drain . . . . marinade from turkey.

Bake . . . . turkey for 8 to 10 hours or until dried into jerky.

Cool . . . . and store in airtight container.

May . . . . bake at 200 degrees for 6 hours if preferred.

The Bromann Family, Glen Ellyn, Illinois

Three-Noodle Soup

2 tablespoons instant chicken bouillon or
6 tablespoons chicken broth powder and 1 teaspoon salt
10 cups water
2 carrots, peeled
2 small zucchini or 1/2 cup frozen peas
4 medium potatoes, peeled
1 cup uncooked narrow noodles
2 cups uncooked medium noodles
1 cup uncooked wide noodles

Tools . . . . measuring spoon, measuring cup, saucepan, spoon, knife, long-handled spoon

Combine . . . . . chicken bouillon and water in saucepan and mix well with spoon.

Slice . . . . carrots. Cut zucchini into halves lengthwise and then slice. Chop potatoes.

Add . . . . vegetables to saucepan.

Bring . . . . to a boil and reduce heat to low.

Simmer . . . . . . for 15 minutes; increase heat.

Add . . . . noodles gradually, stirring with long-handled spoon; reduce heat to medium.

Cook . . . . for 10 minutes or until largest noodles are tender.

Makes . . . . 10 servings.

Mary Murphy, North Canton, Ohio

Italian Vegetable Soup

3 stalks celery, coarsely chopped
1 large onion, chopped
4 carrots, shredded
2 zucchini, shredded
1 or 2 stalks broccoli, chopped
¼ head cauliflower, chopped
2 (15-ounce) cans chopped tomatoes
2 (8-ounce) cans tomato sauce
½ cup dried kidney beans (optional)
8 cups water
½ cup uncooked small macaroni
1 teaspoon parsley flakes
1 teaspoon oregano
1 teaspoon garlic powder
1 teaspoon basil
1 teaspoon salt
1 teaspoon pepper

Tools . . . . knife or salad shooter, can opener, measuring cup, measuring spoon, slow cooker, spoon

Combine . . . . . all ingredients in slow cooker and mix well with spoon.

Cook . . . . on Low for 6 hours or until vegetables are tender.

May . . . . vary vegetables to suit your taste.

Makes . . . . . . 8 servings.

Sarah Meeks, Houston, Texas

Vegetable Chowder

2 cloves of garlic, minced
1 onion, chopped
1 tablespoon olive oil or other oil
2 carrots, peeled, chopped
2 potatoes, peeled, chopped
1/2 teaspoon basil
3 to 4 cups water
1 cup frozen tiny lima beans
1 teaspoon dill
1 cup frozen peas
1 cup frozen corn
Salt and pepper to taste
1 cup evaporated skim milk
Shredded Cheddar cheese

Tools . . . . knife, measuring spoons, saucepan, spoon, measuring cup

Sauté . . . . garlic and onion in heated olive oil in saucepan over medium heat for 2 minutes or until tender.

Add . . . . carrots, potatoes and basil. Sauté for 3 to 4 minutes longer.

Add . . . . water, lima beans and dill and bring to a boil.

Reduce . . . . . . heat. Simmer for 10 minutes.

Add . . . . peas, corn, salt and pepper. Simmer for 5 minutes or until vegetables are done to taste.

Stir . . . . in evaporated milk. Heat just to serving temperature; do not boil.

Sprinkle . . . . . . servings with shredded Cheddar cheese.

May . . . . omit sautéing step if time is short.

Makes . . . . . . 4 servings.

Shlomo Bolts, Miami Beach, Florida

Salad Dressing

1 quart (1 liter) vegetable oil
2 cups (1/2 liter) vinegar
1 cup (245 g) plain yogurt
1 cup (245 g) ricotta cheese
1 tablespoon prepared mustard
Onion, garlic and herbs to taste
1 egg or egg substitute (optional)
3 tablespoons salt or salt substitute

Tools . . . . measuring cup, measuring spoon, blender, jars

Combine . . . . . oil, vinegar, yogurt, ricotta cheese, mustard, onion, garlic, herbs, egg and salt in blender container.

Process . . . . . until smooth.

Store . . . . . . in covered jars in refrigerator.

Serve . . . . over mixed vegetable salad of lettuce, tomatoes, celery, carrots, peppers, mushrooms, broccoli, cabbage, cauliflower or other vegetables of your choice.

Makes . . . . . . 2 quarts.

Heidi Kuonen-Goetz, Switzerland

Baked Chicken

1 to 2 pounds chicken breast fillets
1 bottle steak sauce

Tools . . . . paper towels, baking dish, potholders

Preheat . . . . oven to 350 degrees.

Rinse . . . . chicken and pat dry.

Arrange . . . . in baking dish.

Pour . . . . steak sauce over chicken, coating well.

Bake . . . . at 350 degrees for 45 to 60 minutes.

Serve . . . . with additional steak sauce.

The Meeks Family, Houston, Texas

Dijon Chicken

4 boneless skinless chicken breasts
Salt and pepper to taste
1 tablespoon Dijon mustard
1/4 cup plain yogurt
1/4 cup fine bread crumbs or wheat germ

Tools . . . . baking sheet, measuring cup, measuring spoon, bowl, spoon, potholders

Preheat . . . . . oven to 350 degrees.

Rinse . . . . chicken and pat dry.

Arrange . . . . . in single layer on lightly greased baking sheet.

Sprinkle . . . . . with salt and pepper.

Combine . . . . . mustard and yogurt in bowl and mix with spoon.

Spread . . . . . . over chicken.

Sprinkle . . . . . with bread crumbs.

Bake . . . . for 30 to 45 minutes or until chicken is cooked through.

Makes . . . . 4 servings.

Joyce Thomson, Branford, Connecticut

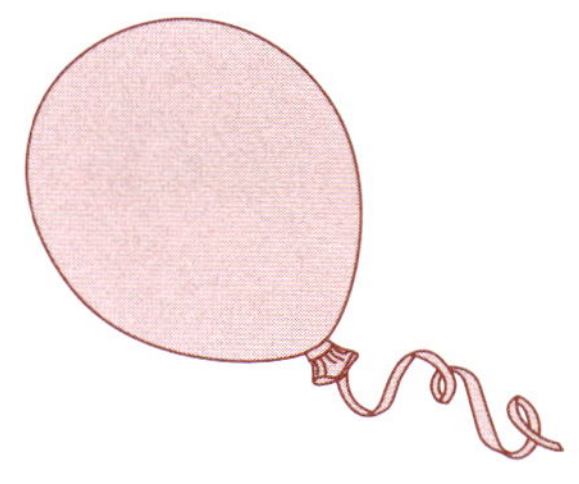

Oven-Fried Chicken

1 egg
1/4 cup milk
1/2 to 1 cup bread crumbs or wheat germ
1/4 teaspoon garlic powder
Salt and pepper to taste
8 boneless skinless chicken breasts

Tools . . . . measuring cup, measuring spoon, bowl, plate, baking dish, fork, potholders

Preheat . . . . . . oven to 400 degrees.

Mix . . . . egg and milk in bowl. Mix bread crumbs, garlic powder, salt and pepper on plate.

Rinse . . . . chicken and pat dry. Dip into egg mixture and then into crumb mixture.

Arrange . . . . . . in baking dish.

Bake . . . . for 45 minutes to 1 hour, turning once with fork.

Makes . . . . 8 servings.

Helen Palmer, Edgewater Park, New Jersey

Painted-Up Chicken

3 to 4 cups corn or wheat flake cereal
1/3 to 1/2 cup grated Parmesan cheese
1/3 to 1/2 cup mayonnaise or plain yogurt
4 chicken breast halves, skinned

Tools . . . . measuring cup, sealable plastic bag, rolling pin, pastry brush, shallow baking pan, fork, potholders

Preheat . . . . . oven to 375 degrees.

Place . . . . cereal in sealable plastic bag and seal.

Crush . . . . with rolling pin.

Add . . . . cheese and shake to mix well.

Rinse . . . . chicken and pat dry.

Paint . . . . with mayonnaise, using pastry brush.

Place . . . . 1 at a time in bag with cereal and shake to coat well.

Arrange . . . . . in shallow baking pan.

Bake . . . . for 45 to 60 minutes or until juices run clear when chicken is pierced with fork.

Makes . . . . 4 servings.

Eileen Puglia, Shoemakersville, Pennsylvania

Tuna Burgers

1 (7-ounce) can tuna
2 tablespoons mayonnaise
1 egg
5 tablespoons rolled oats
Chopped onion and green bell pepper to taste
Wheat germ
Oil

Tools . . . . can opener, measuring spoon, bowl, spoon, skillet, pancake turner

Combine . . . . . tuna, mayonnaise, egg, oats, onion and green pepper in bowl and mix with spoon.

Shape . . . . into patties.

Spread . . . . . . wheat germ on waxed paper.

Place . . . . patties in wheat germ, turning to coat both sides.

Heat . . . . a small amount of oil in skillet. Add patties to skillet.

Fry . . . . until light brown on both sides, turning once with pancake turner.

Serve . . . . on buns with lettuce or sprouts.

Makes . . . . 4 servings.

Karen Herriot, Regina, Saskatchewan, Canada

Pita Pizza

1 cup tomato sauce
2 large cloves of garlic, minced
1 teaspoon oregano
1 teaspoon basil
1 package whole wheat pita bread rounds
1 cup shredded mozzarella cheese
Toppings such as sautéed mushrooms or onions, sliced tomatoes, sliced bell peppers, sliced olives

Tools . . . . measuring cup, measuring spoon, small saucepan, spoon, baking sheet, potholder

Preheat . . . . . oven to 400 degrees.

Combine . . . . . tomato sauce, garlic, oregano and basil in small saucepan and mix well with spoon.

Bring . . . . to a boil and simmer for 10 minutes or until thickened to desired consistency, stirring occasionally.

Arrange . . . . . pita rounds on baking sheet.

Spread . . . . . . sauce on pita rounds.

Sprinkle . . . . . with cheese and favorite toppings.

Bake . . . . for 10 to 15 minutes or until bubbly.

Makes . . . . . . 6 servings.

Joyce Thomson, Branford, Connecticut

I Do It Myself Pizza

1 (15-ounce) can tomato sauce
1 teaspoon basil
1/2 teaspoon oregano
1 tablespoon sugar
2 cloves of garlic, minced
1 recipe Pizza Dough (page 61)
1 cup chopped toppings such as green peppers, red peppers, onions, green onions, mushrooms, or other favorites
2 cups shredded mozzarella cheese, Monterey Jack cheese or Colby cheese

Tools . . . . can opener, measuring cup, measuring spoons, saucepan, spoon, potholders, pizza pan

Preheat . . . . . . oven to 375 degrees.

Combine . . . . . tomato sauce, basil, oregano, sugar and garlic in saucepan and mix well with spoon.

Simmer . . . . . . on stove until bubbly, stirring occasionally.

Spread . . . . . . pizza dough with sauce mixture. Add toppings of your choice.

Sprinkle . . . . . . with cheese.

Bake . . . . at 375 degrees for 20 to 25 minutes or until crust is brown.

May . . . . substitute leftover spaghetti sauce for the cooked pizza sauce.

Cool . . . . for 5 to 10 minutes before cutting into servings.

Makes . . . . . . 4 servings.

Shelley A. Houvener, Warren, Michigan

Pizza Dough

$1\frac{1}{2}$ to 2 cups flour
$\frac{1}{2}$ envelope dry yeast
$\frac{1}{2}$ cup warm water
1 tablespoon vegetable oil

Tools . . . . measuring cup, large bowl, spoon, measuring spoon, electric mixer

Mix . . . . $1\frac{1}{4}$ cups flour and yeast in large bowl with spoon. Add warm water and oil.

Beat . . . . with electric mixer at low speed for 30 seconds and at high speed for 3 minutes.

Stir . . . . in enough remaining flour to form a slightly sticky ball.

Knead . . . . on floured surface for 7 minutes.

Let . . . . rest, covered, for 10 minutes.

Roll . . . . pizza dough to fit pizza pan on floured surface.

Fit . . . . dough into greased pizza pan.

Add . . . . toppings and bake (page 60).

Shelley A. Houvener, Warren, Michigan

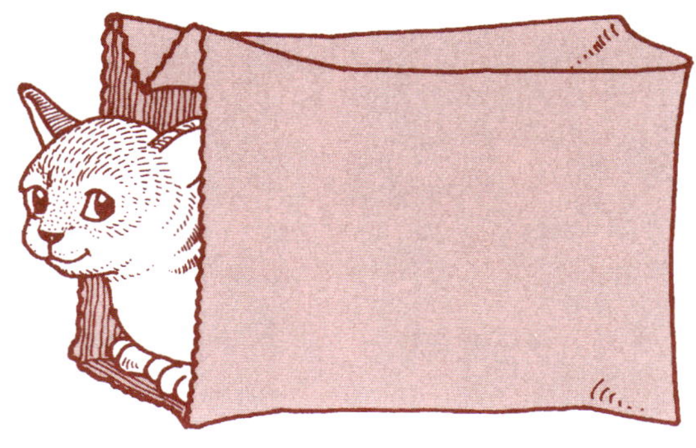

Scrambled Eggs

2 or 3 eggs
1/2 eggshell of milk
Salt and pepper to taste

Tools . . . . bowl, fork, nonstick skillet, spatula, potholder

Combine . . . . . . eggs, milk, salt and pepper in bowl.

Beat . . . . with fork until smooth.

Pour . . . . into nonstick skillet.

Cook . . . . until set, stirring with spatula.

Makes . . . . 2 servings.

The Meeks Family, Houston, Texas

Tamale Bean Pie

1 cup yellow cornmeal
½ teaspoon salt
4 cups water
1 tablespoon vegetable oil
1 small onion, chopped
1 green bell pepper, chopped
2 (16-ounce) cans kidney beans, drained
1 (16-ounce) can chopped tomatoes, drained
1 (12 to 16-ounce) can corn, drained,
or 2 to 3 cups fresh or frozen corn
4 teaspoons chili powder
½ teaspoon salt

Tools . . . . measuring cup, measuring spoons, large heavy saucepan, spoon, large skillet, can opener, 8x12-inch baking dish, potholder

Preheat . . . . . oven to 350 degrees.

Combine . . . . . cornmeal, ½ teaspoon salt and water in large heavy saucepan and mix well with spoon. Cook over low heat for 15 minutes or until very thick, stirring occasionally.

Heat . . . . oil in large skillet over medium heat. Add onion and green pepper. Cook until tender, stirring constantly with spoon. Stir in beans, tomatoes, corn, chili powder and ½ teaspoon salt. Simmer for 5 to 10 minutes, stirring every 2 or 3 minutes.

Spread . . . . . . half the cornmeal mixture in greased 8x12-inch baking dish. Spread bean mixture over cornmeal mixture and top with remaining cornmeal mixture.

Bake . . . . at 350 degrees for 45 minutes or until casserole is bubbly and cornmeal topping is set.

Makes . . . . 8 servings.

Chris Mayou, Onalaska, Wisconsin

Spaghetti Pancake

1/2 cup dried lentils
3 eggs
4 cups cooked spaghetti, about 8 ounces uncooked
1/4 cup milk
1/3 cup shredded Cheddar cheese
1/2 cup frozen peas
1/4 teaspoon oregano
Salt, black pepper and cayenne to taste
Olive oil, butter or margarine
Cinnamon to taste

Tools . . . . measuring cup, colander, saucepan, bowl, fork, measuring spoon, spoon, 10-inch skillet, pancake turner, potholder

Rinse . . . . and sort lentils. Combine with water to cover in saucepan. Cook until tender but not mushy; drain.

Beat . . . . eggs lightly with fork in large bowl.

Add . . . . lentils, spaghetti, milk, cheese, peas, oregano, salt, black pepper and cayenne and mix well with spoon.

Oil . . . . 10-inch skillet with olive oil. Heat over medium-low heat.

Add . . . . spaghetti mixture, pressing down with pancake turner to form pancake. Sprinkle with cinnamon.

Cook . . . . for 10 minutes or until bottom is brown and pancake is firm enough to turn.

Cut . . . . pancake into 4 wedges. Turn 1 wedge at a time with pancake turner. Sprinkle top with cinnamon.

Cook . . . . for 5 minutes longer.

Makes . . . . 4 servings.

Shlomo Bolts, Miami Beach, Florida

Spinach Spaghetti

8 ounces uncooked spaghetti or linguini
1 (10-ounce) package frozen spinach
$^{1}/_{3}$ cup water
Butter and shredded cheese

Tools . . . . saucepan, measuring cup, blender, bowl, spoon, potholder

Cook . . . . spaghetti using package directions; drain and keep warm.

Combine . . . . . spinach with water in saucepan.

Cook . . . . until tender.

Place . . . . spinach and cooking water in blender and process until smooth.

Combine . . . . . spaghetti and spinach mixture in bowl.

Stir . . . . with spoon to mix well.

Serve . . . . with butter and shredded cheese.

Makes . . . . 4 servings.

The Pellegrino Family, Stoughton, Massachusetts

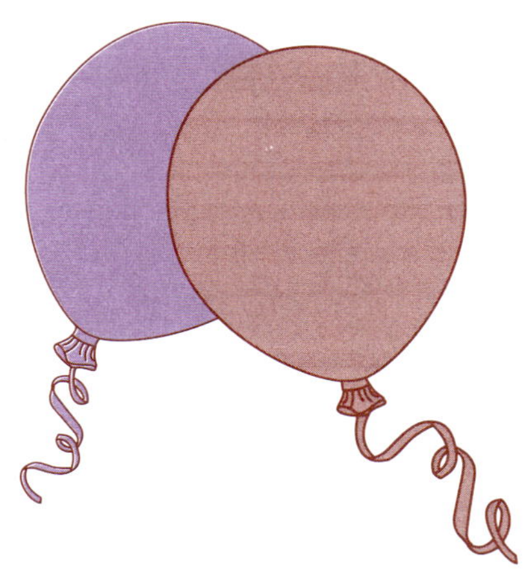

Tropical Lagoon Peas

1 pound fresh or frozen peas
1/4 to 1/2 cup water
1/4 cup slivered almonds
1 (11-ounce) can mandarin oranges, drained
1 or 2 tablespoons butter or margarine
1/4 to 1/2 teaspoon salt
1/8 teaspoon nutmeg

Tools . . . . measuring cup, saucepan, potholder, measuring spoons, can opener, spoon

Cook . . . . fresh peas in water in saucepan for 8 to 12 minutes or just until tender; cook frozen peas using package directions. Drain.

Add . . . . almonds, oranges, butter, salt and nutmeg; mix well with spoon.

Cook . . . . for 1 minute longer.

May . . . . steam peas or cook in microwave if preferred.

Makes . . . . . . 6 to 8 servings.

Chris Mayou, Onalaska, Wisconsin

Potato and Almond Patties

4 to 6 cups mashed cooked potatoes
2 tablespoons butter
1/4 cup ground almonds
1/4 cup slivered almonds
1 teaspoon salt
1/4 teaspoon pepper
1/2 cup ground almonds

Tools . . . . measuring cup, measuring spoons, bowl, spoon, baking sheet, potholder, pancake turner

Preheat . . . . . oven to 400 degrees.

Combine . . . . . potatoes, butter, 1/4 cup ground almonds, slivered almonds, salt and pepper in bowl and mix well with spoon.

Shape . . . . . . into patties or sausage-shaped rolls.

Roll . . . . in 1/2 cup ground almonds, coating well.

Arrange . . . . . on oiled baking sheet.

Bake . . . . at 400 degrees for 30 minutes or until crisp and golden brown, turning after 15 minutes with pancake turner.

Serve . . . . immediately.

May . . . . shape patties and store in refrigerator until needed.

Makes . . . . . . 12 servings.

Chris Mayou, Onalaska, Wisconsin

Squashy Potatoes

Small potatoes
1 pepper squash or other squash
Butter
Salt to taste

Tools . . . . fork, table knife, baking pan, bowl, potholder

Preheat . . . . oven to 400 degrees.

Pierce . . . . potatoes with fork. Cut squash into 4 pieces.

Place . . . . potatoes and squash in baking pan.

Bake . . . . at 400 degrees until tender.

Mash . . . . potatoes and squash with fork in bowl.

Add . . . . butter and salt and mix well.

Karen Golightly, Hamilton, Ontario, Canada

Chilaquiles

6 to 12 stale or dried corn tortillas
Vegetable oil for frying
1/2 onion, chopped
1 tomato, chopped
1 or 2 cloves of garlic, minced
1/4 teaspoon cumin
1 egg
1 (8-ounce) can tomato sauce
1/3 cup shredded Monterey Jack cheese

Tools . . . . table knife, skillet with cover, pancake turner, spoon, measuring spoon, measuring cup, potholder

Cut . . . . each tortilla into 8 wedges or strips with knife or tear into pieces.

Heat . . . . oil in skillet.

Add . . . . tortilla pieces to oil and fry until light brown, turning with pancake turner. Drain all but 1 teaspoon oil from skillet.

Add . . . . onion, tomato, garlic and cumin to skillet.

Cook . . . . for several minutes, stirring with spoon.

Add . . . . egg, stirring to mix well. Stir in tomato sauce and cheese.

Cover . . . . skillet and cook over low heat for 2 to 5 minutes or until done to taste.

May . . . . add more cheese or substitute salsa or enchilada sauce for some of the tomato sauce for a spicier taste.

Makes . . . . 6 to 12 servings.

Beatriz Aguirre Haymer, Honolulu, Hawaii

Brown Rice Patties

3 cups cooked brown rice
3 medium carrots, grated
1 onion, finely chopped
1 egg
1/2 cup whole wheat flour
1/2 teaspoon salt
1/4 teaspoon pepper
1 to 2 tablespoons vegetable oil or butter (optional)

Tools . . . . measuring cup, measuring spoons, large bowl, spoon, skillet, spatula, potholder

Combine . . . . . rice, carrots, onion, egg, flour, salt and pepper in large bowl and mix well with spoon.

Shape . . . . into patties 4 inches wide and 1/2 inch thick.

Heat . . . . oil in skillet over medium heat or spray with nonstick cooking spray.

Add . . . . patties with spatula.

Cook . . . . until patties are light brown on both sides, turning with spatula.

Serve . . . . plain or on bun with mayonnaise and sliced tomato.

May . . . . substitute 1 cup mashed tofu for egg and flour.

Makes . . . . . . 6 servings.

Chris Mayou, Onalaska, Wisconsin

Raisin and Nut Pilaf

1 tablespoon butter or margarine
1 small onion, chopped or 2 tablespoons dried minced onion
3 cups chicken broth or vegetable broth
2 cups uncooked rice
2 tablespoons raisins
$^1/_4$ to $^1/_2$ cup sliced or slivered almonds
Salt and pepper to taste

Tools . . . . measuring spoon, large skillet, spoon, measuring cup, potholder

Heat . . . . butter in large skillet over medium heat.

Add . . . . onion and cook until tender, stirring with spoon.

Add . . . . chicken broth, rice, raisins, almonds, salt and pepper and mix well.

Bring . . . . to a boil and reduce heat.

Cook . . . . for 20 minutes or until liquid is absorbed, stirring occasionally.

May . . . . use brown rice, add 1 more cup chicken broth and cook for 30 to 40 minutes.

May . . . . cook in slow cooker. Use converted rice, 5 cups chicken broth and cook on Low for 6 to 8 hours, stirring occasionally.

Makes . . . . 6 servings.

Chris Mayou, Onalaska, Wisconsin

Flaky Brown Rice

2 cups uncooked brown rice
3 cups water

Tools . . . . microwave-safe bowl with cover, measuring cup, microwave-safe plate

Combine . . . . . rice with water in microwave-safe bowl; cover.

Place . . . . on microwave-safe plate in microwave oven.

Microwave . . . . for 25 minutes or until rice is tender and water is absorbed.

Remove . . . . cover carefully.

Makes . . . . 6 servings.

The Meeks Family, Houston, Texas

Sopa de Arroz

2 tablespoons vegetable oil
1/2 cup uncooked long grain rice
1 clove of garlic, chopped
1/2 onion, chopped
1 celery stalk with leaves, thinly sliced
1 small tomato, chopped
1/4 cup fresh or frozen green peas or mixed vegetables
1/2 teaspoon garlic salt or salt
1 cup chicken broth
1 (8-ounce) can tomato sauce

Tools . . . . measuring spoons, skillet with cover, measuring cup, spoon, can opener, potholder

Heat . . . . oil in skillet over medium heat. Add rice.

Cook . . . . until rice is evenly browned, stirring constantly with spoon.

Add . . . . garlic, onion and celery.

Cook . . . . for 1 minute. Stir in tomato, peas and garlic salt.

Add . . . . chicken broth and tomato sauce; mix well.

Bring . . . . to a boil and cover skillet.

Cook . . . . over low heat for 10 minutes. Do not stir, as this will make the rice gummy.

Turn . . . . off heat and let stand, covered, for 15 to 20 minutes to steam rice.

Makes . . . . 2 servings.

Beatriz Aguirre Haymer, Honolulu, Hawaii

Coffee Cake

1 cup each whole wheat and unbleached flour
1/4 to 1/2 cup packed brown sugar
1 tablespoon baking powder
1/2 teaspoon salt
1 cup water
2 tablespoons vegetable oil
3 tablespoons whole wheat flour
2 tablespoons brown sugar
1 tablespoon butter or margarine, softened
1 teaspoon cinnamon

Tools . . . . measuring cup, measuring spoons, medium bowl, spoon, 8x8-inch baking pan, small bowl, fork, potholder

Preheat . . . . oven to 400 degrees.

Combine . . . . . . 1 cup whole wheat flour, unbleached flour, 1/4 cup brown sugar, baking powder and salt in medium bowl and mix well with spoon. Add water and oil and stir just until moistened.

Spread . . . . in greased 8x8-inch baking pan.

Combine . . . . . . 3 tablespoons whole wheat flour, 2 tablespoons brown sugar, butter and cinnamon in small bowl and mix until crumbly with fork. Sprinkle over coffeecake.

Bake . . . . at 400 degrees for 30 minutes.

Serve . . . . warm or cooled.

May . . . . substitute barley flour for whole wheat flour. If using barley flour in the batter, add 1 teaspoon egg substitute mixed with 2 tablespoons water to the 1 cup water.

Makes . . . . 9 servings.

Tea Biscuits

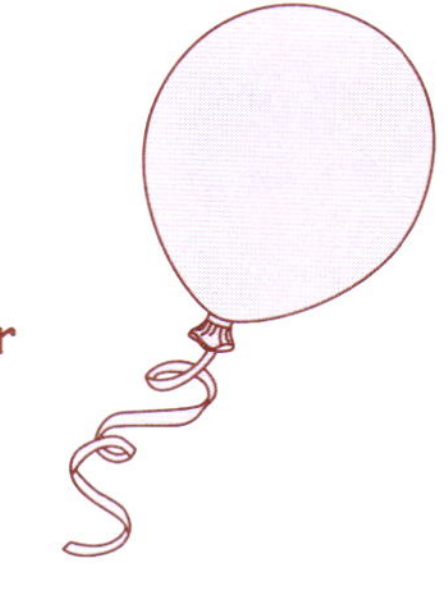

$1^3/_4$ cups flour
$2^1/_4$ teaspoons baking powder
$^1/_4$ cup cold butter
2 eggs
$^1/_3$ cup milk

Tools . . . . measuring cup, measuring spoon, bowl, spoon, 2 knives or pastry blender, fork, muffin tins, potholder

Preheat . . . . . oven to 450 degrees.

Combine . . . . . flour and baking powder in bowl and mix well with spoon.

Cut . . . . in butter with 2 knives or pastry blender until mixture is crumbly.

Add . . . . eggs to milk in measuring cup and mix with fork.

Stir . . . . into dry ingredients until moistened.

Spoon . . . . into muffin cups.

Bake . . . . at 450 degrees for 10 to 15 minutes or until golden brown.

May . . . . substitute $^1/_2$ cup cornmeal for $^1/_2$ cup of the flour. May add currants.

Makes . . . . 8 servings.

Karen Golightly, Hamilton, Ontario, Canada

Apple Pancakes

1 cup whole wheat flour
3/4 teaspoon baking powder
1/2 teaspoon baking soda
1 large egg
1 cup milk or soy milk
1 tablespoon canola oil
1 large Delicious apple, peeled, grated
1/2 teaspoon salt

Tools . . . . measuring cup, measuring spoons, bowl, spoon, griddle, pancake turner, potholder

Combine . . . . . flour, baking powder, baking soda, egg, milk, oil, apple and salt in bowl and mix well with spoon.

Heat . . . . nonstick griddle over medium heat.

Spoon . . . . . . batter onto griddle.

Bake . . . . until golden brown on bottom.

Turn . . . . pancakes with pancake turner.

Bake . . . . until golden brown on remaining side.

May . . . . add additional milk to keep pancakes thin enough to cook apple completely.

Makes . . . . . . 4 servings.

The Bromann Family, Glen Ellyn, Illinois

One-Bowl Pancakes

1$^{1}/_{2}$ cups whole wheat or other flour
1 tablespoon baking powder
$^{1}/_{2}$ teaspoon salt
1 tablespoon butter
1$^{1}/_{2}$ cups milk
2 large eggs

Tools . . . . measuring cup, measuring spoons, bowl, spoon, skillet, fork, pancake turner, potholder

Combine . . . . . flour, baking powder and salt in bowl and mix well with spoon.

Melt . . . . butter in skillet. Add to milk in measuring cup.

Add . . . . eggs to milk mixture and mix well with fork.

Stir . . . . into dry ingredients with spoon.

Heat . . . . skillet over medium heat.

Spoon . . . . batter into hot skillet with ladle.

Bake . . . . until golden brown on both sides, turning with pancake turner.

Makes . . . . 3 servings.

Karen Golightly, Hamilton, Ontario, Canada

Rice Pancakes

1 egg
1/3 cup milk
2 cups cooked rice
1/4 cup whole wheat, barley or rice flour
1 teaspoon sugar or honey (optional)

Tools . . . . measuring cup, bowl, wire whisk, measuring spoon, griddle, spoon, pancake turner, potholder

Whisk . . . . egg and milk together in medium bowl with wire whisk or fork.

Add . . . . rice, flour and sugar and mix well.

Heat . . . . griddle or skillet over medium heat.

Spoon . . . . batter by tablespoonfuls onto griddle.

Bake . . . . until golden brown on both sides, turning with pancake turner.

Serve . . . . hot with favorite topping.

Makes . . . . 4 servings.

Chris Mayou, Onalaska, Wisconsin

Peanut Butter Bread

1/2 cup peanut butter
3/4 cup sugar
1 teaspoon vanilla extract
1 3/4 cups milk
2 1/4 cups whole wheat flour
5 teaspoons baking powder
1/2 teaspoon salt

Tools . . . . loaf pan, measuring cup, measuring spoons, mixer bowl, electric mixer, bowl, spoon, potholders, wire rack

Preheat . . . . . oven to 350 degrees. Grease loaf pan.

Combine . . . . . peanut butter, sugar and vanilla in mixer and beat with mixer until smooth.

Add . . . . milk and mix well.

Mix . . . . flour, baking powder and salt in a bowl. Add to peanut butter mixture and beat until moistened.

Spoon . . . . into loaf pan.

Bake . . . . at 350 degrees for 45 to 50 minutes or until golden brown.

Cool . . . . in pan for 10 minutes. Remove to wire rack to cool completely.

Makes . . . . 12 servings.

Joyce Thomson, Branford, Connecticut

Low-Fat Zucchini Bread

3 eggs
1 cup honey
3/4 cup unsweetened applesauce
1 tablespoon vanilla extract
2 cups whole wheat pastry flour or
1 cup whole wheat flour and 1 cup unbleached flour
1/2 teaspoon baking powder
2 teaspoons baking soda
1 tablespoon cinnamon
1 teaspoon salt
2 cups grated zucchini
1/2 cup nuts, 1/2 cup sunflower seeds, 1 cup raisins (optional)

Tools . . . . 2 large or 3 medium loaf pans, measuring cup, measuring spoons, large mixer bowl, electric mixer, medium bowl, spoon, potholders, wire rack

Preheat . . . . . . oven to 350 degrees. Grease 2 large or 3 medium loaf pans.

Combine . . . . . eggs, honey, applesauce and vanilla in large mixer bowl and beat with mixer until smooth.

Mix . . . . flour, baking powder, baking soda, cinnamon and salt in medium bowl.

Add . . . . flour mixture and zucchini 1/2 at a time to applesauce mixture, stirring with spoon after each addition.

Stir . . . . in desired optional ingredients. Spoon into loaf pans.

Bake . . . . at 350 degrees for 50 to 60 minutes or until golden brown. Cool in pans for 10 minutes. Remove to wire rack to cool completely.

Makes . . . . 24 servings.

Kay Kissinger, Stevens, Pennsylvania

Oatmeal Muffins

1 cup rolled oats
1 cup sour milk
1 egg
1/2 cup honey or packed brown sugar
1 cup whole wheat flour
1 teaspoon baking soda
1/2 teaspoon salt
1/4 cup vegetable oil

Tools . . . . muffin cups, measuring cup, 2 bowls, spoon, measuring spoons, potholders

Preheat . . . . . oven to 400 degrees. Grease muffin cups.

Combine . . . . . oats and sour milk in bowl and mix with spoon. Let stand for 1 hour.

Add . . . . egg and honey and mix well.

Mix . . . . flour, baking soda and salt in bowl. Add to oats mixture and mix well. Stir in oil.

Spoon . . . . into muffin cups.

Bake . . . . at 400 degrees for 15 minutes.

Makes . . . . 12 servings.

Laura Elizabeth Katzer, Grandview, Missouri

Pretzels

1 tablespoon or 1 envelope dry yeast
1 tablespoon sugar
$1\frac{1}{2}$ cups lukewarm water
4 cups flour
1 egg, beaten
Coarse salt to taste

Tools . . . . baking sheet, measuring spoon, measuring cup, large bowl, spoon, brush, potholder

Preheat . . . . . . oven to 425 degrees. Grease baking sheet.

Combine . . . . . yeast and sugar in large bowl and mix well with spoon.

Test . . . . water on wrist; it should feel the same temperature as your skin, no warmer or cooler. Add to yeast mixture and mix well.

Stir . . . . in flour.

Knead . . . . with hands until dough feels smooth.

Tear . . . . off small pieces of dough and shape as desired; use your imagination to make animals, letters or numbers.

Place . . . . on greased baking sheet.

Brush . . . . with beaten egg and sprinkle with salt.

Bake . . . . at 425 degrees for 15 minutes or until brown.

Makes . . . . . . 16 servings.

Heidi Gleber, East Bloomfield, New York

Baked Apples

2 baking apples
2 tablespoons butter or maple syrup
1 teaspoon butter or cold-pressed canola oil
1 cup hot water

Tools . . . . apple corer, baking dish, measuring spoons, measuring cup, fork, potholder

Preheat . . . . . oven to 375 degrees.

Remove . . . . . core of apples with apple corer, leaving bottoms intact.

Place . . . . apples in baking dish.

Spoon . . . . 1 tablespoon honey into hole in each apple.

Add . . . . 1/2 teaspoon butter and a sprinkle of cinnamon to each.

Pour . . . . water around apples.

Bake . . . . covered, at 375 degrees for 45 minutes or until apples test tender with fork.

Serve . . . . warm.

Makes . . . . 2 servings.

The Bromann Family, Glen Ellyn, Illinois

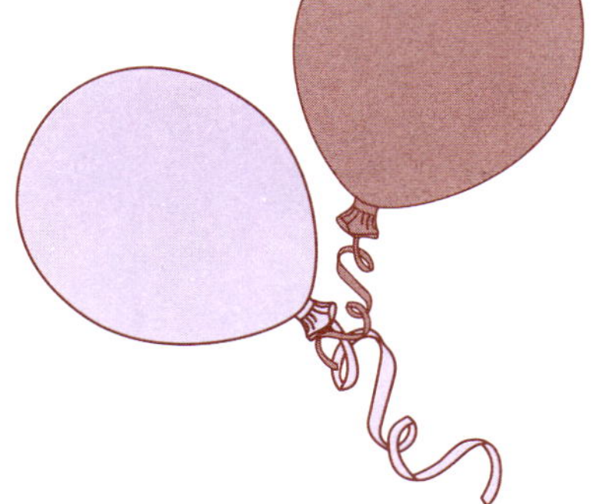

Naturally Sweet Apple Crisp

1/2 cup rolled oats
6 tablespoons thawed frozen apple juice concentrate
6 cups sliced peeled cooking apples
2 tablespoons instant tapioca
1 1/2 teaspoons cinnamon
1/2 teaspoon nutmeg
1/4 teaspoon salt
1 cup thawed frozen apple juice concentrate
1/2 cup whole wheat or barley flour
1/2 teaspoon cinnamon
1/4 cup butter, softened

Tools . . . . measuring cup, measuring spoons, 3 bowls, spoon, 8x8-inch baking pan, pastry blender, potholders

Preheat . . . . . . oven to 375 degrees.

Combine . . . . . oats and 6 tablespoons apple juice concentrate in bowl and mix well with spoon. Set aside for topping. Place apple slices in 8x8-inch baking pan.

Combine . . . . . tapioca, 1 1/2 teaspoons cinnamon, nutmeg and salt in medium bowl and mix well with spoon. Stir in 1 cup apple juice concentrate. Pour over apples and mix lightly to coat well.

Mix . . . . flour and 1/2 teaspoon cinnamon in bowl. Add butter and mix with pastry blender until mixture is crumbly. Add oats mixture and mix lightly. Sprinkle over apple mixture and press down lightly.

Bake . . . . at 375 degrees for 35 minutes. Serve warm or cooled with whipped cream or ice cream.

May . . . . make in slow cooker. Reduce apple juice in apple mixture to 3/4 cup and cook on Low for 4 to 6 hours.

Makes . . . . 9 servings.

Chris Mayou, Onalaska, Wisconsin

Pull-Out-A-Plum Crisp

2 cups chopped peeled plums
2 to 4 tablespoons honey
1 cup Grape Nuts cereal
1/4 teaspoon cinnamon
1 teaspoon butter or cold-pressed oil

Tools . . . . pie plate, measuring cup, measuring spoons, potholders

Preheat . . . . . oven to 350 degrees. Grease pie plate.

Place . . . . plums in pie plate.

Drizzle . . . . with honey.

Sprinkle . . . . . with cereal and cinnamon and mix lightly.

Dot . . . . with butter.

Bake . . . . at 350 degrees for 25 minutes.

Put . . . . in a spoon, pull out a plum, and say "What a good cook am I!"

Makes . . . . 6 servings.

The Bromann Family, Glen Ellyn, Illinois

Bread Pudding

$2\frac{1}{2}$ cups milk
3 to 4 cups dried whole grain bread cubes
$\frac{1}{2}$ cup honey
1 teaspoon vanilla extract
$\frac{1}{2}$ teaspoon salt
2 eggs
Lemon Sauce (page 87)

Tools . . . . measuring cup, measuring spoon, medium saucepan, potholders, spoon, fork, small bowl, 2-quart baking dish

Preheat . . . . oven to 350 degrees. Grease 2-quart baking dish.

Heat . . . . milk in medium saucepan over medium heat just until it starts to steam; do not boil. Remove from heat.

Add . . . . bread to milk and mix well with spoon. Set aside.

Combine . . . . . honey, vanilla and salt in small bowl and mix well with spoon.

Beat . . . . eggs with fork in small bowl. Add to honey mixture and mix well.

Add . . . . to bread and milk and mix gently with spoon.

Spoon . . . . into baking dish.

Bake . . . . at 350 degrees for 1 hour.

Spoon . . . . into serving dishes.

Top . . . . with Lemon Sauce.

Makes . . . . 8 servings.

Chris Mayou, Onalaska, Wisconsin

Lemon Sauce

1 cup hot water
$^{1}/_{4}$ cup honey
$1^{1}/_{2}$ tablespoons lemon juice
2 tablespoons butter
Nutmeg and salt to taste

Tools . . . . measuring cup, measuring spoon, saucepan, spoon

Combine . . . . . hot water, honey, lemon juice, butter, nutmeg and salt in saucepan and mix well with spoon.

Cook . . . . over medium-high heat until thickened, stirring constantly.

Serve . . . . over Bread Pudding (page 86).

Makes . . . . 8 servings.

Chris Mayou, Onalaska, Wisconsin

Applesauce Oatmeal Cake

1/2 cup packed brown sugar or molasses
2 eggs
3 cups unsweetened applesauce
2 1/2 cups whole wheat or barley flour
2 teaspoons baking soda
2 teaspoons cinnamon
1/2 teaspoon each ground cloves, mace and allspice
1 1/2 cups rolled oats
1/2 cup raisins

Tools . . . . 9x13-inch cake pan, measuring cup, large bowl, wire whisk, measuring spoon, large spoon, cake tester, potholders, wire rack

Preheat . . . . . . oven to 350 degrees. Grease 9x13-inch cake pan.

Combine . . . . . brown sugar and eggs in large bowl and whisk until smooth. Whisk in applesauce.

Sift . . . . flour, baking soda, cinnamon, cloves, mace and allspice into medium bowl. Add to applesauce mixture and mix well with spoon.

Stir . . . . in oats and raisins.

Pour . . . . into cake pan.

Bake . . . . at 350 degrees for 30 to 35 minutes or until a cake tester inserted into center comes out clean. Top will be higher than sides and center may crack.

Cool . . . . in pan on wire rack or serve warm.

Serve . . . . with strawberries and whipped cream or frost with cream cheese frosting.

Makes . . . . . . 15 servings.

Chris Mayou, Onalaska, Wisconsin

Tropical Carrot Cake

2 eggs
1/3 cup honey
2 1/2 cups whole wheat flour or barley flour
2 teaspoons baking soda
1/4 teaspoon salt
3/4 cup chopped walnuts or almonds
1 1/2 cups unsweetened crushed pineapple with juice
1 cup shredded carrot
1/2 cup unsweetened shredded or flaked coconut

Tools . . . . tube or bundt pan, measuring cup, mixer bowl, electric mixer, measuring spoon, spoon, cake tester, potholders, wire rack

Preheat . . . . . . oven to 350 degrees. Grease tube or bundt pan. Sprinkle with about 2 tablespoons flour and tip to coat well, shaking out excess.

Combine . . . . . . eggs and honey in mixer bowl and mix well with electric mixer. Add flour, baking soda and salt and mix well.

Stir . . . . in walnuts, undrained pineapple, carrot and coconut.

Spoon . . . . into cake pan.

Bake . . . . at 350 degrees for 35 to 40 minutes or until cake tester inserted in center comes out clean.

Cool . . . . in pan on wire rack.

Invert . . . . onto serving plate.

May . . . . frost with cream cheese frosting or whipped cream.

Makes . . . . 16 servings.

Chris Mayou, Onalaska, Wisconsin

Oat Bran Fruit Bars

3/4 cup rolled oats
3/4 cup whole wheat or barley flour
3/4 cup oat bran
2 tablespoons vegetable oil, softened butter or softened margarine
1/2 cup unsweetened applesauce
1/3 cup packed brown sugar
2 tablespoons honey
1/4 cup finely chopped walnuts or almonds (optional)
3/4 teaspoon cinnamon
1 teaspoon vanilla extract
1 1/2 cups fruit-only jam

Tools . . . . 8x8-inch baking pan, measuring cup, measuring spoons, medium bowl, spoon, potholders, wire rack, table knife

Preheat . . . . . . oven to 375 degrees. Grease 8x8-inch baking pan.

Combine . . . . . oats, flour, oat bran, oil, applesauce, brown sugar, honey, walnuts, cinnamon and vanilla in medium bowl and mix well with spoon or hands.

Pat . . . . a little more than half of the mixture into 8x8-inch baking pan.

Spread . . . . . . with jam.

Sprinkle . . . . . . with remaining oats mixture and press down lightly.

Bake . . . . at 375 degrees for 20 to 25 minutes or until top is brown.

Cool . . . . in pan on wire rack.

Cut . . . . into bars with knife.

Makes . . . . 18 servings.

Chris Mayou, Onalaska, Wisconsin

Oatmeal Squish Cookies

1 cup butter, softened
1 cup packed brown sugar
1 egg, slightly beaten
2 teaspoons vanilla extract
1 cup all-purpose flour
1/2 cup whole wheat flour
1/2 teaspoon baking soda
1/2 teaspoon cinnamon
1/2 teaspoon salt
1 1/2 cups rolled oats
3 tablespoons wheat germ (optional)
1/2 cup semisweet chocolate chips or carob chips
1/2 cup raisins

Tools . . . . measuring cup, mixer bowl, electric mixer, measuring spoons, medium bowl, spoon, cookie sheets, glass, potholders, wire rack, pancake turner

Preheat . . . . . oven to 350 degrees.

Combine . . . . . butter and brown sugar in mixer bowl and beat with electric mixer until smooth. Beat in egg and vanilla.

Mix . . . . flours, baking soda, cinnamon and salt in medium bowl. Add to butter mixture and mix until smooth.

Stir . . . . in oats, wheat germ, chocolate chips and raisins.

Drop . . . . by tablespoonfuls onto cookie sheets.

Squish . . . . each cookie to 1/4-inch thickness with bottom of glass dipped in flour.

Bake . . . . at 350 degrees for 8 minutes.

Cool . . . . on cookie sheets on wire rack for 2 minutes. Remove with pancake turner to wire rack to cool completely

Makes . . . . 3 dozen.

Julia Parker, Shawnigan Lake, British Columbia, Canada

Old-Fashioned Raisin Bars

1 cup raisins
1 cup water
1/2 cup butter or margarine
1 cup sugar
1 egg
1 3/4 cups flour
1 teaspoon baking soda
2 1/2 teaspoons cinnamon
1/2 teaspoon nutmeg
1/4 teaspoon salt

Tools . . . . 9x13-inch baking pan, measuring cup, saucepan, spoon, measuring spoon, medium bowl, potholders, wire rack, table knife

Preheat . . . . . . oven to 375 degrees. Grease 9x13-inch baking pan.

Combine . . . . . raisins and water in saucepan.

Bring . . . . to a boil and remove from heat.

Stir . . . . in butter with spoon. Cool to lukewarm. Add sugar and egg and mix well.

Sift . . . . flour, baking soda, cinnamon, nutmeg and salt into medium bowl. Add to raisin mixture and mix well.

Spoon . . . . into 9x13-inch baking pan.

Bake . . . . at 375 degrees for 20 minutes.

Cool . . . . in pan on wire rack.

Cut . . . . into bars with table knife.

Makes . . . . 3 dozen.

Laura Elizabeth Katzer, Grandview, Missouri

Blueberry Pie

1/4 cup melted butter
1 cup graham cracker crumbs
1 cup (250 millileters) whipping cream
1/4 cup sugar
2 cups (500 grams) plain yogurt
1 (4-serving) package vanilla instant pudding mix
Fresh blueberries

Tools . . . . measuring cup, bowl, spoon, 8-inch pie plate, deep bowl, electric mixer

Combine . . . . . butter and graham cracker crumbs in bowl and mix well with spoon.

Press . . . . . . into 8-inch pie plate.

Beat . . . . whipping cream in a deep bowl with electric mixer for 5 minutes.

Add . . . . sugar and beat until soft peaks form.

Add . . . . yogurt and mix well.

Stir . . . . in dry pudding mix.

Spoon . . . . . . into pie shell.

Chill . . . . in refrigerator.

Spoon . . . . . . blueberries over top.

Chill . . . . for 5 minutes.

Makes . . . . . . 6 servings.

May . . . . substitute other fruit for blueberries. May make in 8x8-inch square dish.

Graham Boyes, Vancouver, British Columbia, Canada

Index

About La Leche League

La Leche League International is a nonprofit organization founded in 1956 by seven women who wanted to make breastfeeding more rewarding for mother and child.

La Leche League offers information and encouragement primarily through personal help to those women who want to nurse their babies. A Professional Advisory Board offers advice and assistance when necessary.

La Leche League is the world's largest resource for breastfeeding and related information. **The Womanly Art of Breastfeeding**, a basic how-to book, has helped countless mothers through almost any breastfeeding situation.

For further information, we urge you to locate a La Leche League Group in your area. If you don't find a listing in your telephone book, write or call our LLLI Headquarters in Schaumburg, Illinois, during regular business hours from 8 AM to 5 PM Central Time. The number is (708) 519-7730.

LA LECHE LEAGUE INTERNATIONAL
1400 North Meacham Road
Post Office Box 4079
Schaumburg, Illinois 60168-4079

The Womanly Art of Breastfeeding
Includes information on correct positioning, working and breastfeeding, jaundice in the breastfed baby, breastfeeding after a cesarean birth, and the latest research on the physical, psychological and emotional benefits of breastfeeding. All of this information, combined with the warmth and support of stories from mothers who are breastfeeding today, make **The Womanly Art of Breastfeeding** a must for any woman who plans to breastfeed. Available in softcover from local La Leche League Groups and bookstores everywhere.

You may purchase additional copies of **Whole Foods for Kids to Cook** and companion volumes, **Whole Foods for the Whole Family** and **Whole Foods from the Whole World**, from the nearest La Leche League Group, your local bookseller, or from La Leche League International.